California

CALIFORNIA REPUBLIC

A Buddy Book
by
Julie Murray

ABDO
Publishing Company

VISIT US AT

www.abdopub.com

Published by ABDO Publishing Company, 4940 Viking Drive, Edina, Minnesota 55435.

Printed in the United States.

Edited by: Sarah Tieck
Contributing Editor: Michael P. Goecke
Graphic Design: Deb Coldiron, Maria Hosley
Image Research: Sarah Tieck
Photographs: Acclaim Images, Corbis, Getty Images, Medio Images, One Mile Up, Photodisc, Photos.com

Library of Congress Cataloging-in-Publication Data

Murray, Julie, 1969-
    California / Julie Murray.
        p. cm. — (The United States)
    Includes bibliographical references and index.
    ISBN 1-59197-664-2
        1. California—Juvenile literature. I. Title.

F861.3.M87 2005
979.4—dc22
                                                                2004046120

Table Of Contents

A Snapshot Of California

California is a sunny state. This is one reason why people call California "The Golden State." There are many other reasons for California's nickname.

The golden poppy became the state flower in 1890.

One is that the state was named for a magical, golden island. This island was described in a Spanish novel by Garci Rodríguez de Montalvo in the 1500s.

In 1849, many people came to California as part of the gold rush. The state's flower is the golden poppy. Today, California is also called golden because many famous movie stars live there.

There are 50 states in the United States. Every state is different. Every state has an official state nickname.

California was a United States territory first. This happened when the war with Mexico ended in 1848.

When gold was discovered, more and more people moved to California. They wanted to make California an official state. California became the thirty-first state on September 9, 1850.

California has about 158,648 square miles (410,896 sq km) of land. It is the third-largest state in the United States. Only Alaska and Texas are bigger. More people live in California than in any other state in the nation. More than 33 million people call California home.

Many people live and work in California. This state has the largest population.

Where Is California?

There are four parts of the United States. Each part is called a region. Each region is in a different area of the country. The United States Census Bureau says the four regions are the Northeast, the South, the Midwest, and the West.

Four Regions of the United States of America

ALASKA

WASHINGTON

MONTANA

NORTH DAKOTA

OREGON

IDAHO

MINNESOTA

WISCONSIN

VERMONT

MAINE

NEW HAMPSHIRE

MASSACHUSETTS

NEW YORK

RHODE ISLAND

CONNECTICUT

WYOMING

SOUTH DAKOTA

MICHIGAN

PENNSYLVANIA

NEW JERSEY

DELAWARE

NEVADA

UTAH

COLORADO

NEBRASKA

IOWA

ILLINOIS

INDIANA

OHIO

WEST VIRGINIA

VIRGINIA

Washington D.C.

MARYLAND

CALIFORNIA

KANSAS

MISSOURI

KENTUCKY

NORTH CAROLINA

ARIZONA

NEW MEXICO

OKLAHOMA

ARKANSAS

TENNESSEE

SOUTH CAROLINA

MISSISSIPPI

ALABAMA

GEORGIA

TEXAS

LOUISIANA

FLORIDA

HAWAII

West   Midwest   South   Northeast

The state of California is located in the West region of the United States. The weather in California is usually warm. Trees are green, and flowers bloom all through the year there.

A view of a California coast on the Pacific Ocean.

California has unique borders. The entire western coast of California is on the Pacific Ocean. The country of Mexico is to the south. California is also bordered by three states. Oregon is north. Nevada and Arizona lie to the east.

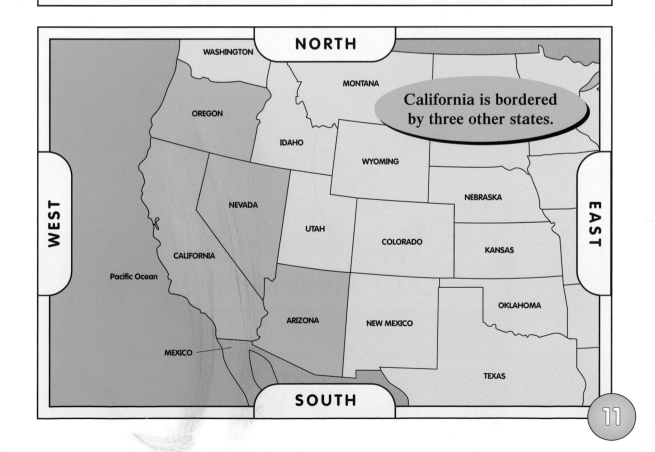

California is bordered by three other states.

California

State abbreviation: CA

State nickname: The Golden State

State capital: Sacramento

State motto: Eureka! ("I have found it!")

Statehood: September 9, 1850, 31st state

Population: 33,871,648, ranks 1st

State flag:
Adopted in 1911

CALIFORNIA REPUBLIC

Land area: 158,648 sq mi (410,896 sq km), ranks 3rd

State tree: California redwood

State song: "I Love You, California"

State government: Three branches: legislative, executive, and judicial

Average July temperature:
75°F (24°C)

Average January temperature:
44°F (7°C)

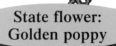

State flower:
Golden poppy

State animal:
Grizzly Bear

State bird:
California valley quail

Cities And The Capital

Los Angeles is the largest city in California. It is the second-largest city in the United States. More than 3.5 million people live in Los Angeles. Los Angeles is in southern California. It is on the Pacific Ocean.

The city of Los Angeles.

The Hollywood sign is a famous landmark in California.

Los Angeles is known for having art and culture. The city is filled with writers, actors, musicians, and artists. Some of these people are movie stars. Hollywood is part of Los Angeles. Many television shows and movies are made there.

San Diego is California's second-largest city. San Diego is located at the southern tip of California. Spanish soldiers founded this city in 1769. Some people call San Diego the birthplace of California.

Today, San Diego is known for its natural deepwater harbor. This harbor is part of San Diego Bay. The San Diego Zoo is also there. It is one of the largest zoos in the world.

The city of San Diego is on San Diego Bay.

San Francisco is another major city in California. This city is home to the famous Golden Gate Bridge. It is known for having some of the hilliest streets in the world. People ride cable cars up these steep hills.

A view of San Francisco.

The Golden Gate Bridge.

Sacramento is the capital of California. It is located in northern California. Sacramento's capitol building was completed in 1874. It has a glass dome on the top.

The California State Railroad Museum is also in Sacramento. It is one of the largest railroad museums in the world.

The capitol building is in Sacramento.

Famous Citizens

Julia Child (1912–2004)

There are many famous people from California. Julia Child was one. She was a famous chef, writer, and television personality. She was born in Pasadena in 1912. Julia hosted one of the first television cooking shows in 1963. The show was called *The French Chef*. She also wrote many books on cooking.

Julia Child

Famous Citizens

Richard Milhous Nixon (1913–1994)

Richard Milhous Nixon was born in Yorba Linda in 1913. He was president of the United States from 1969 to 1974. He was the thirty-seventh president.

Richard Nixon was known for his work with other countries. He helped end the Vietnam War and the military draft. He was the first president to visit China. He also visited the Soviet Union. And, he was the first president ever to resign from office. This happened in 1974.

President
Richard Nixon

Golden Gate Bridge

The Golden Gate Bridge is located in San Francisco. It is a suspension bridge. This means that the bridge hangs on two steel cables. The cables are very thick. The cables hang from two towers. The towers are 746 feet (227 m) above the water.

Millions of people cross the Golden Gate Bridge each year.

The Golden Gate Bridge is 8,981 feet (2,737 m) long. It is one of the longest suspension bridges in the world.

The name of the bridge comes from the waterway that runs under the bridge. This waterway is called the Golden Gate Strait. It connects the Pacific Ocean to the San Francisco Bay.

Fog covers the Golden Gate Bridge and the San Francisco Bay.

Giant Trees

California is home to the tallest trees in the world. These trees are called coast redwood trees. They grow along California's north and central coast.

Redwood trees grow to more than 300 feet (90 m) tall. Their trunks can be 8 to 12 feet (2 to 4 m) wide. The tallest known redwood tree stands more than 367 feet (112 m) high.

This large redwood tree is in Redwood National Forest.

A sequoia tree.

One species of redwood is the sequoia. Sequoia means "big tree." The world's largest tree is a giant sequoia tree. This tree has the most wood of any tree in the world. It measures 274 feet (84 m) tall. The base is more than 100 feet (30 m) around. It is called the "General Sherman Tree." It is in Sequoia National Park.

Death Valley

Death Valley is located in southeastern California and Nevada. Pioneers and gold seekers named Death Valley around 1849. It got its name because many people died crossing through the dry, hot land. Death Valley also has mountains, cliffs, canyons, and a volcano.

Death Valley has extreme landscape elevation.

This area is known for extreme temperatures. Summer temperatures are well over 100° Fahrenheit (38° C). A temperature of 134° Fahrenheit (57° C) was recorded in Death Valley in 1913. That is the hottest temperature ever recorded in the United States. Winter temperatures often drop below freezing.

Death Valley is also the lowest point in the Western Hemisphere and the United States. Badwater, in Death Valley, is 282 feet (86 m) below sea level.

Red Pass is located in Death Valley.

Death Valley is dry like a desert.

California

1542: Juan Rodríguez Cabrillo arrives. He is one of the first explorers in California.

1769: Spain claims land in California.

1821: Mexico becomes independent from Spain. California becomes part of Mexico.

1846: People in California declare independence from Mexico. The people in California begin to fight to be part of the United States.

1848: The war with Mexico ends. California becomes a territory of the United States.

During the Gold Rush, people used pans to search for gold. This was called "panning."

1849: The Gold Rush begins. This was a time when many people came to California to find gold.

1850: California becomes the thirty-first state of the United States on September 9.

1854: Sacramento becomes the state capital.

1863: Construction of the Central Pacific Railroad starts in Sacramento. This was the start of the first railroad to cross the United States.

1869: Railroad tracks are completed. California was linked to the East Coast by these tracks.

1874: The capitol building is completed in Sacramento.

1906: An earthquake and a fire destroy San Francisco.

1994: Los Angeles experiences the most powerful earthquake in the city's history. Some freeways collapse. There are 57 deaths and $20 billion in damage.

2003: Actor Arnold Schwarzenegger becomes the 38th governor of California.

Cities in California

★ Sacramento

● Stockton

San Francisco ●
● Oakland

Sunnyvale ● ● San Jose

● Fresno

Pasadena
● ● San Bernardino
Los Angeles ● ● Riverside
Long Beach ● Yorba Linda

● San Diego

Important Words

capital a city where government leaders meet.

independent to be free from the rules of another.

nickname a name that describes something special about a person or a place.

strait a narrow waterway connecting two larger bodies of water.

suspension bridge a bridge that hangs from cables.

territory an area of the United States that is not yet an official state.

unique being the only one of its kind.

Web Sites

To learn more about California, visit ABDO Publishing Company on the World Wide Web. Web site links about California are featured on our Book Links page. These links are routinely monitored and updated to provide the most current information available.

www.abdopub.com

31

Index